FAITH

Samuel Ward

Adapted and Paraphrased from
The Sermons of Samuel Ward by
Richard Rushing

THE BANNER OF TRUTH TRUST

THE BANNER OF TRUTH TRUST
3 Murrayfield Road, Edinburgh EH12 6EL, UK
P.O. Box 621, Carlisle, PA 17013, USA

*

© The Banner of Truth Trust, 2008

ISBN-13: 978 0 85151 980 7

*

Typeset in 10.5 / 13.5 pt Adobe Caslon Pro
at the Banner of Truth Trust, Edinburgh

Printed in the USA by
Versa Press, Inc.,
East Peoria, IL

PART ONE

THE LIFE OF FAITH

The Just Shall Live by His Faith

Man once had a happy life in the Garden of Eden, living in the image and favour of his Creator, but after the Fall what vain pursuits he craves to restore his happiness! He is like the Sodomites groping at Lot's door, or the blind leading the blind in a maze of error. The covetous, when he is blessed with goods, applauds his soul as if he has received that which is truly good. The sensual, when he is satisfied with the husk of pleasure, cries out that he is living a royal and happy life. The ambitious, when he has climbed the steep and slippery hill of honour, thinks he is in the highest sphere of happiness. Alas! Do not all of these know they are in the chambers of death? They are dead while they are alive! They are walking ghosts in the form of living men. If one of them lives a hundred years, begets children, plants crops and builds grand buildings, and yet sees no other good but this, it would be better not to have lived at all!

There are many by-paths you might tread in life, but only one true way to happiness. There are many errors, but only one grand truth. Consider, each of you who are looking into the ways of life, what Christ said: 'I am the way, the truth, and the life.' He came from heaven to vanquish death, and by His death has brought life to you. He only has the words of everlasting life. Look at true happiness, in the case of the life of Paul. Did not his life after his conversion display a constant course of joy? Certainly his happiness, even while he lived in the flesh, came about because he lived by faith in the Lord Jesus Christ (*Gal.* 2:20). Come, each of you, therefore, who desires to see good days, and lay hold of the ways of life by faith in Christ, for 'the just shall live by his faith' (*Hab.* 2:4; *Rom.* 1:17; *Gal.* 3:11; *Heb.* 10:13). Faith is the doorway to the power of God, first to save us, and then to strengthen us. By faith we lay hold of the tree of life that heals us from our sin. 'Blessed is the man whose sin is covered' (*Psa.* 32). Through faith we are strengthened; 'I can do all things through him who strengthens me.' By faith we have a life of joy and comfort, cheering the soul in the midst of all trials and tribulations. Thus, Job in the valley of death, exulted and trusted in his living Redeemer, and Paul in the midst of calamities was more than a conqueror (*Rom.* 8:37). May we not truly say that faith supplies abundantly all things pertaining to life and godliness?

Oh faith! When I read of you, when I meditate on you, when I feel any part of your virtue, I find you to be a wonder-worker. I consider nothing but high and honourable things of you. But when I look into the world, and upon the lives of those who call themselves believers, I begin to question my own thoughts and dreams. Faith in them is but a name, a sound, a mere word, and not a powerful thing. Why are so many of Christ's followers so dead, so dull, and so melancholy? Why are men of the world more merry and as righteous as these? Has faith's strength faded? Is its virtue exhausted in these latter days? Is it because men do not truly know it? Paul of old, and Luther of late, teach of the greatness of faith, but the world does not understand it, or does not apply it.

Faith finds its lustre in action, and not just in notion. It enters our hearts and not just our heads. This is the difference between one who reads about pleasant rivers and high mountains and one who travels to visit them. What a difference there is between understanding the notion of sweetness, and actually tasting honey or sugar. In a word, you see schools disputing it, preachers preaching it, professors discussing it, profane men swearing by it, but few or none living by it. This is like a rich man that lives like a miser without the benefit of his money. It is possible for a man to have a gift of God and not the use of it. Among all the gifts of God, there is nothing more useful than faith. It is profitable for this life and the life to come. It is profitable for all parts and purposes of our lives. The uses of it are manifold, and rich in every possible way.

Faith, the Door to Salvation

Let me begin with those who are at the door of salvation. You realize that you are dead in sin and desire to place your trust in Christ and live. The law has wounded you and you are reaching to the gospel for healing. You struggle as to whether you have faith or not. You desire to come into the light but seem to struggle to do so. Why do you not come right out of darkness and into the land of the living? Allow faith to do her perfect work in you, and to form Christ in your heart. Do not allow yourself to be delayed in the power of fear and doubt. Three common causes may keep you in the snares of death:

1. *You would believe, but you know that you have been a sinner.* But is it not sinners Christ came to save? Does not Scripture say that he justifies the ungodly? Oh, you say, but my sins are scarlet, crying, scandalous sins! Did not Christ say that all things are possible to faith, if you only believe? Are not all your faults easily pardonable by infinite mercy? Did not Christ's blood wash David's bloody sin as white as snow? Does he not delight to forgive much, that we might love much? Will not his favour

abound to you in your faith as your sin has abounded in the wounding of your heart? Oh, you say, but I am an old habitual sinner. Did Christ come from heaven to cure only small scars and cuts? Are not the deep serious wounds that are longstanding included? He can cast out, not only solitary devils, but legions also! Oh take heed, and take your eyes off yourself and look upon Christ. No matter how deadly your sting might be, by mere looking, by only believing, you shall be cured and live!

2. *You can easily be deceived by pride that comes in the clothing of humility.* Like Peter, will you refuse to allow Christ's precious hand to wash your foul feet? Was not Christ well pleased with the humble Canaanite woman who accepted the name of dog, and

was willing to receive even the crumbs from the master's table? It is high pride not to come when you are called. Faith is obedience. The sooner you come, the better the welcome. It is rudeness, and not good manners, not to come when you are called! To do the work of God is to believe on him that the Father has sealed and sent to be the Saviour (*John* 6).

3. *You would like to repent first, mend your ways, do some good works, and then you might be bold to come.* You feel you will not be welcome unless you come with your payment. You would accept his pardon if you could pay for it. But he bids you to come and buy without silver. Otherwise, he says, may you and your money perish! Did Christ come to a prior agreement with Zaccheus

concerning restitution? Did Paul bid the jailor to become a new man, and then believe? No! Faith comes first. Swim out of these weeds, and lay hold on the Rock, Christ. And to bring forward your birth by the act of believing, set before your eyes Christ's welcome, in the days of his flesh, to all who truly desired the price of his blood!

Study, strive, and endeavour to believe, as you do with something difficult to understand. Pray for the ability to believe. Today is salvation offered! Step from death to life, and write this day as your birthday. Mark it as the beginning of your life. By faith you are a child of God for ever! A mark of true faith is a new purpose, desire and resolution to obey. But Zaccheus, the jailor, and all new converts, had no more than this as their warrant: 'Believe, and you shall be saved!'

Faith and Young Christians

By faith put off your sackcloth and ashes, and put on the garments of joy and gladness! Let your clothes be white, and anoint your head with oil. Live, I say! Live today, live tomorrow, live, O Christian, forever! This you may do if you learn to use your faith. Not like your wedding clothes that you use, and then put away for special occasions only.

Use your faith always, as a necessity, as you use fire, water, salt, bread, wine, or other necessities. Faith is not just the midwife to bring you into joy and peace, and then you may let it go. It is more like a nurse or foster mother to bring you on to full maturity in them. Faith is even sweeter in its mature fruit than in its beginings. Do you desire to have a continual feast, and to rejoice always in the Lord? I know you do desire it with all your soul. Let me prescribe a daily regime to be strictly kept (may the Lord give both you and me grace to keep it). Just as often as you refresh your body by food and recreation, cheer up your soul by using your faith. Let your soul have two or three walks each day up to Mount Tabor, that is, to some retired place of meditation and prayer, like Isaac's field, Cornelius's walks, or David's closet.

What is to be done there? Faith is to be put to use! This is the chief mystery of our spiritual life. Stir up your soul in this mountain to talk with Christ. Consider all the promises and privileges you regularly enjoy. Now actually think of them, roll them under your tongue, chew on them until you feel their sweetness in the palate of your soul. View them together and individually. Sometimes contemplate one in particular, or another more deeply.

Consider how wonderful it is that your debts have been cancelled, and that the wrath of God has been satisfied. Consider how happy and safe a condition you are in by being a son of God, and how pleasant a state not to fear death and hell. Consider how stately a thing it is to be an heir of glory. Mingle these thoughts with your prayers to heaven for grace and aid. Do not leave the mountain until your heart has been cheerfully warmed and revived in strength for the next day.

This is using your faith. It is living by faith. You will find your soul saying, with good reason, 'It is good to be here.' It is good to be here daily, to come here often! The fire in unstirred coals does not glow, and does not heat the house. Sugar unstirred in the cup does not sweeten the wine. Not using your faith is almost as bad as not having it at all.

What good does a lock do you if you do not have the key? It is not owning land, but also tilling and planting that provides food. Oh, that we could see this truth as clearly in the matter of faith as in the ordinary affairs of life! The principal benefit and beauty of faith is in its use, and not in the bare possession of it. The more you exercise your body, the more you can do. The more liberally a man gives alms, the more his liberality grows and shines. The use of faith breeds victory. Through disuse things perish and come to nothing. The plough, laid up, will rust and disintegrate, but employed it will shine, do great good, and last much longer. Let a man diligently and thoroughly make use of his faith and it will become great, and great will be the joy that it will bring to him.

PART TWO

*THE FOLLY OF
NEGLECTING FAITH*

*L*ive by faith; again I say, always live by it. Always rejoice through faith in the Lord! It is neglecting this exercise that allows your own low moods and Satan to interrupt your happiness and spiritual cheerfulness and to hold you in the dumps and in gloominess. What if you have a natural inclination to melancholy? Cannot faith correct nature? Does it not have power to clear the mind of all cares, fears and griefs? Can it not exhilarate the whole man? But what good is this faith if it is not used? It is like a soldier, with a sword at his side, not drawing his weapon when he is attacked. If a discouragement overtakes, cannot your faith say to your soul, 'Why are you disturbed? Know and consider in whom you believe.' Would not the master rebuke the winds and the storms and bring calm to your mind again? Do not most men have something they use to counteract their discouragements, like David with his harp? Some seek refreshment in company, or wine, or tobacco. They would not go far without a supply of these! But would not the least taste of faith be far better?

Should not the wise Christian rather take in the sweet air from the precious promises of God? Keep your faith, and it will keep your joy. It will keep it in an even, ever-flowing current, without ebb and flow, clouds or eclipses, turning ever upon the hinges of heavenly and solid joy. How can it be otherwise?

Do not Christians consider how unsuitable it is for them to go about drooping and hanging the head? Is it not becoming for the righteous to rejoice? What is a Christian but one who is joyful? Does not the kingdom of heaven consist in joy? Does not heaviness drive people away while joy draws and wins? Men wonder to see a rich man, who has all his heart's desire, in a fit of heaviness. But I wonder a thousand times more to see one that has Christ as his friend, and God as his shepherd, and knows that all must work for the best, to be any time out of tune or out of sorts. For a Nabal to be as dead as a stone is no surprise to me, but if Nehemiah's countenance is changed, there must be some extraordinary cause.

Can you be sad when you have all possible treasures laid up in heavenly places, where moth and rust and thieves may not come? Our treasures are out of the devil's reach, and not only for a number of years, but for ever and ever!

O vain man! Show me your faith by your joy. If you say you have faith and live a life of sadness, I will not believe you. Use your faith, and have joy; increase your faith and increase your joy.

Faith and a Mature Christian

I must now draw you a little higher. It is a small thing for you to be cheerful at an ordinary level. Your joy should exceed the happiness of those in the world both in quantity and quality. If your joy is not sweeter, and higher, and more pure, more constant than that of a carnal man, you dishonour your faith and show you are young in the kingdom of heaven, which is joy unspeakable and full of glory in the Holy Spirit. Do you not have living water flowing out of your soul? Should you that have tasted of the grapes of Canaan, pine for the onions and garlic of Egypt? Do you need to stoop to the world's puddle to drink when you have tasted faith's sweet fruits?

Certainly God gives us ordinary and lawful delights in the world, the wine and oil, music, recreations, etc. These God allows us to enjoy for the sake of bodily health, but not to stuff ourselves with them. We enjoy them, but we can be happy without them. We do not live for them, but live by faith.

It is sad to see a Christian pursuing joy in coarse and earthly pleasures when he has more noble and angelical delights, second only in degree and manner of enjoyment to heaven itself. Our faith takes us to the third heaven. We roll and tumble our souls in beds of roses, that is, our meditations of justification, sanctification, and salvation through Christ. No day should pass without these enjoyments. Should not our soul have her due drinks, breakfasts, meals, snacks, and desserts, as well as our body? Cannot such meditations make pleasant work of our daily tasks? They would make time pass by like a boat with full wind and tide, needing no oars. They would make all of our days like holidays and celebrations.

Faith and Failure

You will reply, 'The exercise of our faith would be possible and easy if it were not for our failures that dampen our joy. How can faith not be damped by such stumbling?'

The answer is this: he who daily keeps watch with his God shall seldom or never fall into any foul slough, or dash the ship of his faith against a dangerous rock. If he does, his faith will soon make him go out, weep bitterly, make peace between the Lord and his conscience, and restore his joy and fellowship. For his ordinary infirmities his faith will daily secure his pardon, washing, and scouring his soul every morning and evening even more than a Pharisee washes his hands. He will daily draw the red lines of Christ's cross over the black lines of God's debt-book. Does not God himself, who knows all things, and sees the violations of his law much better than we, even every act of sin in thought, word or deed, look upon the handwriting against us, and see the bills paid in full and cancelled with the precious blood of his Son! This blood is sufficient to cover, nullify, abolish, and wholly take away our sins, in such a way that he neither sees, will see, nor can see them as requiring action against us!

Some suggest that such a doctrine will encourage sinners to go on in sin, if pardon is so great. Oh, peevish and perverse generation! The text does not say that every hypocrite and profane professor of faith shall live by his faith, but the righteous. These promises are only ministered to prepared and true believers. These pearls are not for swine. They are reserved for the true bride of Christ alone. Our text implies that whoever believes and lives by his faith must also of necessity be a righteous man, not just imputatively, but also in himself. One that loves righteousness, that denies and hates unrighteousness, and seeks daily to be more and more righteous, deserves to be labelled righteous, though not perfectly.

How Faith Sanctifies and Mortifies

Holiness is a natural and necessary effect of faith. Consider all that Christ has done for you. Consider how he has forgiven you so many debts and conferred so many favours of all kinds upon you. Is there anything you can do to repay such love? If you give all your goods to the poor, or give your body to be burned, or your whole life to his service, this is not enough to repay. Do you love your Saviour? Do you dare to do anything that is displeasing to him? Is there anything too good, too hard or dear for him?

Mary, if your tears might wash his feet, would you hesitate to pour them out? Is your hair too good to be his towel? Is there any spikenard too costly for his head? Joseph, the Lord has need of your tomb, will you deny him? Zaccheus, do you love your wealth above him who saved you? Stephen, do you love your life above your Master? Does not faith constrain us more than all wages and prizes? Does it not get more from us than any torture or punishment?

So that when you want to get anything out of your wayward heart, set your faith to work, and you will be sure to obtain it. The power of God will secretly empower your heart, infusing it with a pliable willingness, and making your will lamb-like, and dove-like. All this it does by fetching its efficacy from the life and death of Christ, from that mighty power whereby Christ raised himself from the dead, cured all the diseases, and performed his miracles. This transforms the heart of man, and creates new principles of action in him. Prove this power in the mortifying of your flesh to sin, and in making your spirit alive to holiness.

Do you find a strong inbred, habitual vice troubling you and keeping you prisoner against your will? Have you often resolved to forsake it, but failed? Have you tried purposing, promising, resolving, vowing, fasting, and watching? By faith, touch but the hem of his garment! You shall feel virtue come from him to cure your disease. But you must die to yourself and renounce the broken reed of your own power, which has often deceived you. Place all your trust in the grace of Christ, and it will crucify the old man. Be weak in yourself and strong in the Lord, and by faith you shall be more than a conqueror. Leave struggling with your sin, and fall, with Jacob, to wrestling with Christ for a blessing. Though you go limping away, you shall be a prince with God and be delivered from Esau's bondage.

What if Satan with his legions has long held possession in some strong fort of your heart, persist in resisting, and he shall fly and you shall see him fall like lightning before you.

Christ raised not only the daughter of Jairus that had just died, but also Lazarus who had been in the grave four days, so that those long dead in sin, stinking in the nostrils of the world need not despair. Through faith you can set your feet on the neck of the kings that have tyrannized over you, and triumph over them. Faith can cure diseases that are beyond all other cures and hopes.

PART THREE

FAITH GIVES ABUNDANT LIFE

*F*aith can do even more for you. Do you say that it is not enough to be healed of your disease unless you may also take up your bed and walk? 'Oh, that I could find the life of grace which I have seen in some. Their meat and drink is to do the will of God!' One might say, 'Though I am not pestered and mastered by any reigning corruption, yet I find myself dull and backward so that I take no pleasure in my life. Prayer, meditation, and enjoyment of the Lord's day are about as easy as iron swimming or stones flying.' But nothing is impossible to faith! It can make these things natural to you. This is how David came to delight in God's service. He loved the commandments of God more than thousands of gold and silver pieces, and they were sweeter to him than the honeycomb. He rose at midnight to meditate in the things of his God. The natural man may carry out many of these duties, but not from a heart of faith. Faith makes them go smoothly and flowingly and makes our yoke light and easy. They that trust in the Lord shall renew their strength, they shall run and not grow weary, they shall walk and not faint (*Isa.* 40:31).

Faith draws nourishment from the root, Christ, which makes every tree bring forth fruit according to its kind. This taught David to fight, Paul to preach, and Onesimus to be a faithful servant. See what a full treasury of all graces Christ has stored up within him. Faith draws from this.

It opens the tap to water all the herbs and flowers in the garden. Many seek to perfect this or that virtue, but without the root virtue of faith! He who trusts in the Son honours the Father most. Faith can make us as meek as Moses, as patient as Job, as zealous as David. Our soul and life can be embroidered with all kinds of shining graces. When you are on top of Mount Tabor, comforting your soul in the Lord, and seeking his favour through faith, feasting and banqueting with him as Esther with Ahasuerus, think what to ask him, what enemy you would be rid, such as some great Haman of pride. Consider what grace you need and ask for your portion as Achsah did to Caleb (*Judg.* 1:14).

Follow this instruction daily, even though some days you will be more fervent than others, as the Spirit assists you. I do not promise you that you will arrive at perfection, yet as you grow from faith to faith, so shall you grow from strength to strength in his graces, till by degrees you will attain to maturity in Christ. You will be a saint upon the earth. You will be a light in this dark world. You will be able to live in holiness and righteousness all the days of your life, with much more comfort to yourself and credit to the gospel than strangers to the life of faith think possible.

Faith Upholds Our Life in Affliction

Is there anything still lacking that prevents the complete happiness of a believer's life, that faith cannot supply? The flesh (which is ever cowardly and loves ease) is not happy at the poverties, crosses, and pressures it must endure. But here faith shines and triumphs over nature and reason, not merely as a sufferer, but more than a conqueror and victor, rejoicing in tribulations! Faith can make you like an adamant stone that nothing can break, like a palm that does not sink under the heaviest of burdens, like oil that rises above the greatest quantity of water that can be poured over it, or the sheet anchor that holds when all other tackling breaks. This is the crown and glory of faith.

Faith tackles great obstacles. Small boats do well in calm conditions, ordinary men can stand up to a light breeze, but when a heavy tempest blows, and wave after wave crashes in, nature yields, spirits faint, hearts fail. To stand up against such storms and to live and reign is the work of faith, which has the Word as its compass, and Christ at the helm. The greatest adversities are but the exercise and lustre of faith. Men glory when they can tame tigers and lions, make the elephant bow to them, and the bear to follow them. But what a small conquest is that compared with faith when it makes shame, poverty, sickness, persecution, banishment, yea, death itself, to be not only not dreadful, but manageable and bearable. A Christian has great advantage because of his faith. His only defect is a lack of skill or a failure to use the shield of faith when a dart comes suddenly at him. Therefore when a storm rises, immediately run and awaken your sleeping faith. Knock at faith's door! Say, 'Faith! Now do your work!' Consider these five remedies that faith will offer for your relief:

1. Faith will confidently assure you of this ground of comfort: not the slightest trouble befalls you without the overruling eye and hand, not only of a wise God,

but of a tender Father and a sympathizing Saviour. They know what you are made of, and measure out every cross as precisely as chemists measure out minute amounts of dangerous medicines.

2. Faith will draw out these infallible conclusions: this trouble is not the axe of destruction, but the pruning knife of affliction; not to poison but to heal, no matter how bitter the taste. Whatever befalls you as a Christian cannot lead to your condemnation or utter overthrow, but there will be a way out of it. Though the storm make a terrible noise over your head, it will be like hailstones on a roof that rattle more than hurt. You are kept by the power of his might, and the evil one shall not touch you. You are in a safe harbour under the

rock Christ. You know in whom you have trusted and you will never be confounded. Sickness or poverty are in your Father's own hand. If the rod comes from a malicious enemy, your Father stands by, looks on, and will moderate and number the blows. The devils could not go one inch beyond the command to enter the herd of swine. God knows your strength and will not permit more to be laid on you than you are able to bear. His wisdom and grace shall be sufficient for you. He that is good friends with the king does not fear the approach of a herald. He that is out of debt does not fear the court, and he considers the approach of the bailiff to bring good news.

3. Faith will further assure you that God not only restrains your crosses, but has

determined that they will bring the greatest benefit possible to you! He sends them to purge, refine, try, and exercise you, but they will produce the quiet fruit of righteousness. The affliction will bring the best possible results. When you feel your heart sinking for the present, remember you will be better afterwards. Though, with Job and David, your flesh is troubled, and grunts and groans, after you have come through it you will say; 'Oh, this was good for me!' If your Father should deal indulgently with you, he would hate you, and not love you.

4. Faith will moreover remind you that Christ is your partner in affliction. What if your cross is heavy, and you a weak child? Christ is strong and bears the greater part of the burden. When Stephen was stoned,

Christ said to Saul, 'Why are you persecuting *me*?' This is a proof of your sonship, to be like him, not yet in glory, but as he was on the way to glory, when he despised the shame, the spitting, buffeting and taunts. He showed himself the Son of God, not by coming down from the cross, but by enduring it. If you wish to be his disciple, the first lesson in his school is Christ's cross. Deny yourself, take it up, and follow him; and glory with the martyrs, 'Now I am like my Lord and Master.'

5. Lastly, faith will set before you the infinite reward, the eternal weight of glory that is to come. Paul, in the light of this, counted his afflictions light and momentary in comparison. This made him not only not weep and howl in the dungeon,

but sing, counting it a special honour and favour to be not only a believer but a sufferer for Christ. The apostles chose rather to be in Christ's garrison with torments than in the palaces of princes. The more hazard and peril, the more glory and honour. What could we desire more than to die daily, that the life of Christ may be manifested in us? Even in the very instant of death, faith so helps the believer that he may be said not to see death, and never to die! If all the complaints, grievances, wants, and miseries of life are rightly weighed, the cause of them is either lack of faith or failure to practise faith.

So that we can conclude with that worthy ensign-bearer of Christ, John Foxe, 'By faith we stand, by faith we fight, by faith we overcome.'

PART FOUR

*A FINAL ENCOURAGEMENT
TO THE EXERCISE OF FAITH*

*L*et me now ask the reader a question or two. *How many do you know that truly live by their faith?* Does not the common man even doubt the existence of such sweetness in the life of faith, because he does not see believers more cheerful and contented than others? Is it not true that if tradesmen worked in their trade as most Christians practise their faith, they would end up beggars!

Forgetting others however, let me ask you a more profitable question: *Do you yourself live by your faith?* This week, or yesterday, how did you spend the day? What were your thoughts in the morning? What did you drink for your soul and heart's nourishment? What was it that made you happy when you were alone and in company? Was entertainment and food of greater joy than your heavenly meditations? Deal plainly with yourself in this matter. This discourse, will witness against you, if you refuse to put it into practice. Have you spent half an hour, or fifteen minutes, in exercising your faith? Have you been troubled about many things, and allowed the only needful thing to be forgotten? Have you wasted a day, or a week, or the month past, and starved your soul of this refreshment?

I fear this for many of my readers. How much more for those who generally are not readers at all? If this is true of you, let your heart smite you for this folly. Slap yourself on the thigh, and say 'Oh, how I have lived, or rather not lived, and wasted precious days in time-consuming vanities!'

Recover and come to your senses before you go hence and be no more. Will you die before you have lived? Oh, learn to live this life of faith, for it is never too late! I am sure also that it is never too soon! It is no shame to learn to live at the age or condition that you are. If you are a prince, ruler, nobleman, or gentleman, learn to live! No matter how honourable, prosperous, pleasurable, or great you may be, this is not true happiness. True pleasure is only in a life of faith. What is a Christian without his faith? What is life without the use of faith?

If you are a scholar or a preacher, what is your work? Is it not this life of faith? What is Paul or Apollos but instruments through whom you believed? If you have taught anything without this, you might as well have spoken to the chairs and stones of the building. Are not your hearers but dead bones until they believe and have Christ formed in them? Show yourself to be a skilful workman, and raise them from their spiritual deadness. The word of faith is the arm and power of God to the salvation of every believer. Above all let us live by that faith we encourage others to live by. Is it not a shame that we do not live more happily and carefully by our faith than those we lead? Do we not have an advantage over these in that this is our life's work? If we do not advance before others in our faith, it is a shame to us.

This life of faith is available to all. The poorest among us, and the least educated can travel this road to heaven. The poor may have little opportunity to become wealthy or honourable, but they can live a truly happy life through faith! They can live such a life just as much as the greatest princes and learned educators. Whoever you are, if you desire to lift up your condition and change the few days of your pilgrimage into happier and longer days, faith is the art of living well and living long!

Life is not numbered by its hours, but by its cheerfulness. Money is not valued by the number of coins, but the value of the coins. It takes many silver coins to match the value of a gold coin. Is not one week in health better than a year in a crazed state? Is not one hour of bright sunshine better than a day of gloom? To live well, is to live twice. A good man doubles and amplifies his days. One day lived by the rules of faith is better than an immortality of vanity. A man may live in as much contentment to himself and others for a short time as others do in a long life. Some are old in years tediously drawn out, and others in hours cheerfully spent. Living by faith is to enjoy, like the king of Israel, a continual portion, a kingly portion, all the days of our life (2 *Kings* 25:30). I conclude with *one caution, one piece of advice, and one request.*

First, *do not think that I am speaking of absolute perfection in this life.* We will not have that until the life to come. Certainly now we have all things in part, and imperfectly. Even by assiduous reading, prayer, and meditation, we cannot have God's Spirit at our absolute command, any more than mariners the wind, or the farmer the showers. Even the most observant believer has his buffetings, so that he may seek God more eagerly, prize his presence more thankfully, hold to him more carefully, and trust more in his grace. Yet, though this is true, he who daily puts his faith into practice will be blessed more with the gusts and gales of the Spirit, with the restraint of Satan from frequent attacks, with fewer long and tedious absences of the Spirit, and with a more steady and consistent joy and comfort than a negligent believer. He will have a more constant experience of joy than any other kind of man in the world that does not take this course.

Secondly, as to advice, *seal up your senses and chain up your reason*. Walk by faith and not by sight. Close up the eye of your soul to worldly things. Fix your spiritual eye upon heavenly delights. You do not need to go out of the world or into a hermit's seclusion from society, but even in the midst of the glittering objects that would draw your gaze, see them as if you did not see them; that is, without being deeply affected by them. Moses, when he was in Pharaoh's court, fixed his eye upon him who is invisible. A sound believer goes through the world like a man whose mind is in deep thought, or like one who has an errand of great importance. He walks down a street looking at nothing, hearing nothing, and considering nothing but that with which his mind is taken up. Our conversation, our treasure is in heaven. Oh, that all our thoughts were there, in such a way that no earthly object might detain or distract us, except in what is necessary for our calling, and that our main bent and intention might be the daily nourishing of our faith!

My closing request is that you should determine and resolve in your heart not to let one day pass (God helping you by his Spirit), in which you may set aside at least a quarter of an hour one or two times a day to withdraw from all company to seek the strengthening of your faith. That is, that you may, by prayer, reading, and meditation put strength and life into your faith, till you have cheered, revived, and warmed your soul. If you shall observe this faithfully, the strength, feeling, comfort, and fruits of your faith will little by little thrive and grow until you arrive at maturity in Christ.

You should fully purpose to do this every day of your life. While you are in the world, live by your faith. While others make much ado about needless trifles, build yourself up in your most holy faith. So live by faith in the darkness of this world, until the time when you will be fully satisfied with all good things in their perfection at the right hand of God, when our faith will be turned into sight.

These things I have written that your joy may be full. 'The just shall live by his faith.' 'According to your faith be it done unto you.' 'Lord, increase our faith.'

MEMOIR OF SAMUEL WARD

J. C. Ryle
(1862)

Samuel Ward is comparatively unknown to most readers of English theology. This is easily accounted for. He wrote but little, and what he wrote has rarely been reprinted. How far his writings deserve this neglect, I am content to leave to the judgment of all impartial students of divinity into whose hands the volume of his

Sermons[1] may fall. But I venture the opinion, that it reflects little credit on the discretion of republishers of old divinity that such a writer as Samuel Ward has been virtually passed over.

As a Suffolk minister, and a thorough lover of Puritan theology, I should have been especially pleased, if it had been in my power to supply full information about Samuel Ward. I regret, however, to be obliged to say that the materials from which any account of him can be compiled are exceedingly scanty, and the facts known about him are comparatively few.

Nor yet, unhappily, is this difficulty the only one with which I have had to contend. It is an unfortunate circumstance, that no less than three divines named 'S. Ward'

[1] 1636, 1862; reprinted Edinburgh: Banner of Truth, 1996 (196 pp., clothbound).

lived in the first half of the seventeenth century, and were all members of Sydney (now Sidney Sussex) College, Cambridge. These three were, Dr Samuel Ward, Master of the College, one of the English commissioners at the Synod of Dort, and a correspondent of Archbishop Usher; Seth Ward, who was successively Bishop of Exeter and Salisbury; and Samuel Ward of Ipswich, the author of these sermons. The two 'Samuels' were undoubtedly the most remarkable men; but the similarity of their names has hitherto involved their biographies in much confusion. I can only say that I have done my best, in the face of these accumulated difficulties, to unravel a tangled skein, and to supply the reader with accurate information.

The story of Samuel Ward's life is soon told. He was born at Haverhill, in Suffolk,

in the year 1577, and was eldest son of the
Rev. John Ward, minister of the gospel in
that town.[2] He was admitted a scholar of

[2] John Ward, the father of Samuel Ward, appears to have been
a man of considerable eminence as a minister and preacher. Fuller
(in his *Worthies of Suffolk*) says that the three sons together would
not make up the abilities of their father. The following inscription
on his tomb in Haverhill church is well worth reading:

JOHANNES WARDE
Quo si quis scivit scitius,
Aut si quis docuit doctius,
At rarus vixit sanctius,
Et nullus tonuit fortius.

Son of thunder, son of ye dove,
Full of hot zeal, full of true love;
In preaching truth, in living right, –
A burning lampe, a shining light.

LIGHT HERE.   STARS HEREAFTER.

John Ward, after he with great evidence
and power of ye Spirite, and with much fruit,
preached ye gospel at Haverill and Bury in
Suff. 25 yeares, was heere gathered to his fathers.
Susan, his widdowe, married Rogers, that worthy
WATCH.   Pastor of Wethersfielde. He left 3 sonnes,   WARDE.
Samuel, Nathaniel, John, Preachers, who for

St John's College, Cambridge, on Lady Margaret's foundation, on Lord Burghley's nomination, November 6, 1594, and went out B.A. of that house in 1596. He was appointed one of the first fellows of Sydney Sussex College in 1599, commenced M.A. 1600, vacated his fellowship on his marriage in 1604, and proceeded B.D. in 1607.

Nothing is known of Ward's boyhood and youth. His entrance on the work of the ministry, the name of the bishop by whom he was ordained, the date of his ordination, the place where he first began to do Christ's work as a preacher, are all things of which apparently there is no record. His

---

them and theirs, wish no greater blessing
than that they may continue in beleeving
and preaching the same gospel till ye coming
of Christ. Come, Lord Jesus, come quicklye.
WATCH.   Death is our entrance into life.   WARDE.

first appearance as a public character is in the capacity of lecturer at his native town of Haverhill. Of his success at Haverhill, Samuel Clark (in his *Lives of Eminent Persons,* p. 154, ed. 1683), gives the following interesting example, in his life of Samuel Fairclough, a famous minister of Kedington, in Suffolk:

God was pleased to begin a work of grace in the heart of Samuel Fairclough very early and betimes, by awakening his conscience by the terror of the law, and by bestowing a sincere repentance upon him thereby, and by working an effectual faith in him; and all this was done by the ministry of the word preached by Mr Samuel Ward, then lecturer of Haverhill. Mr Ward had answered for him in baptism, and had always a hearty love to him. Preaching one day on the conversion of Zaccheus, and discoursing upon his fourfold restitution in cases of rapine and extortion, Mr Ward used that frequent expression, that no man can expect pardon from God of the wrong done to another's estate, except he make full restitution to the wronged person, if it may possibly be done. This was as a dart directed by the hand of God to the heart of young Fairclough, who, together with one John Trigg, afterwards a famous physician in London, had the very week before robbed the orchard of one Goodman Jude of that town, and had filled their pockets as well as their bellies with the fruit of a mellow pear tree.

At and after sermon, young Fairclough mourned much, and had not any sleep all the night following; and, rising on the Monday morning, he went to his companion Trigg and told him that he was going to Goodman Jude's, to carry him twelve pence by way of restitution for the three pennyworth of pears of which he had wronged him. Trigg, fearing that if the thing were confessed to Jude, he would acquaint Robotham their master therewith, and that corporal correction would follow, did earnestly strive to divert the poor child from his purpose of restitution. But Fairclough replied that God would not pardon the sin except restitution were made. To which Trigg answered thus: 'Thou talkest like a fool, Sam; God will forgive us ten times, sooner than old Jude will forgive us once.' But our Samuel was of another mind, and therefore he goes on to Jude's house, and there told him his errand, and offered him a shilling, which Jude refusing (though he declared his forgiveness of the wrong), the youth's wound smarted so, that he could get no rest till he went to his spiritual father Mr Ward, and opened to him the whole state of his soul, both on account of his particular sin and many others, and most especially the sin of sins, the original sin and depravation of his nature. Mr Ward received him with great affection and tenderness, and proved the good Samaritan to him, pouring wine and oil into his wounds, answering all his questions, satisfying his fears, and preaching Jesus to him so fully and effectually that he became a true and sincere convert and dedicated and devoted himself to his Saviour and Redeemer all the days of his life after.[3]

[3] I think it right to remark that Clark, in all probability, has erred in his dates in telling this story. He says that Fairclough was born in 1594, and that the event he has recorded took place when he was thirteen years old. Now, in 1607 Ward had ceased to be lecturer of Haverhill. Whether the explanation of this discrepancy is that Fairclough was born before 1594, or that he was only nine years old when he stole the pears, or that Ward was visiting at Haverhill in 1607 and preached during his visit, or that Fairclough was at school at Ipswich and not Haverhill, is a point that we have no means of deciding.

From Haverhill, Samuel Ward was removed, in 1603, at the early age of twenty-six, to a position of great importance in those days. He was appointed by the Corporation of Ipswich to the office of town preacher at Ipswich, and filled the pulpit of St Mary-le-Tower, in that town, with little intermission, for about thirty years. Ipswich and Norwich, it must be remembered, were places of far more importance four hundred years ago, than they are at the present day. They were the capital towns of two of the wealthiest and most thickly peopled counties in England. Suffolk, in particular, was a county in which the Protestant and evangelical principles of the Reformation had taken particularly deep root. Some of the most eminent Puritans were Suffolk ministers.

To be chosen town preacher of a place like Ipswich, four hundred years ago, was a very great honour, and shows the high estimate which was set on Samuel Ward's ministerial character, even when he was so young as twenty-six. It deserves to be remarked that Matthew Lawrence and Stephen Marshall, who were among his successors, were both foremost men among the divines of the seventeenth century.

The influence which Ward possessed in Ipswich appears to have been very considerable. Fuller says, 'He was preferred minister *in*, or rather *of*, Ipswich, having a care over, and a love from, all the parishes in that populous place. Indeed, he had a magnetic virtue (as if he had learned it from the loadstone,[4]

[4] I suspect that Fuller's remarks about the loadstone refer to a book, called *Magnetis Reductorium Theologium*, which is sometimes attributed to Samuel Ward of Ipswich. But it is more likely that the authorship of this book belongs to Dr Samuel Ward,

in whose qualities he was so knowing) to attract people's affections.' The history of his thirty years' ministry in the town of Ipswich, would doubtless prove full of interesting particulars, if we could only discover them. Unhappily, I can only supply the reader with the following dry facts, which I have found in an antiquarian publication of considerable value, entitled, *Wodderspoon's Memorials of Ipswich*. They are evidently compiled from ancient records, and throw some useful light on certain points of Ward's history. Wodderspoon says:

> In the year 1603, on All-Saints' day, a man of considerable eminence was elected as preacher, Mr Samuel Ward. The corporation appear to have treated him with great liberality, appointing an hundred marks as

---

the Principal of Sydney College, of whom mention has already been made.

his stipend, and also allowing him £6:13:4 quarterly in addition, for house rent.

The municipal authorities (possibly, because of obtaining so able a divine) declare very minutely the terms of Mr Ward's engagement. In his sickness or absence he is to provide for the supply of a minister at the usual place three times a week, 'as usual hath been.' 'He shall not be absent out of town above forty days in one year, without leave; and if he shall take a pastoral charge, his retainer by the corporation is to be void. The pension granted to him is not to be charged on the foundation or hospital lands.'

In the seventh year of James 1, the corporation purchased a house for the preacher, or rather for Mr Ward. This house was bought by the town contributing £120, and the rest of the money was made up by free contributions, on the understanding that, when Mr Ward ceased to be preacher, the building was to be re-sold, and the various sums collected returned to those who contributed, as well as the money advanced by the corporation. In the eighth year of James I, the corporation increased the salary of Mr Ward to £90 per annum, 'on account of the charges he is at by abiding here'.

In the fourteenth year of James I, Mr Samuel Ward's pension increased from £90 to £100 yearly.

The preaching of this divine, being of so free and puritanic a character, did not long escape the notice of the talebearers of the court; and after a short period, spent in negotiation, Mr Ward was restrained from officiating in his office. In 1623, August 6th, a record appears in the town books, to the effect that 'a letter from the king, to inhibit Mr Ward from preaching, is referred to the council of the town'.

About the remaining portion of Ward's life, Wodderspoon supplies no information. The little that we know about it is gleaned from other sources.

It is clear, from Hackett's life of the Lord Keeper Bishop Williams (p. 95, 1693 ed.), that, though prosecuted by Bishop Harsnet for nonconformity in 1623, Ward was only suspended temporarily, if at all, from his office as preacher. Brook (in his *Lives of the Puritans,* vol. 2, p. 452), following Hackett, says, that

> upon his prosecution in the consistory of Norwich, he appealed from the bishop to the king, who committed the articles exhibited against him to the examination of the Lord Keeper Williams. The Lord Keeper reported that Mr Ward was not altogether blameless, but a man easily to be won by fair dealing; and persuaded Bishop

Harsnet to take his submission, and not remove him from Ipswich. The truth is, the Lord Keeper found that Mr Ward possessed so much candour, and was so ready to promote the interests of the church, that he could do no less than compound the troubles of so learned and industrious a divine. He was therefore released from the prosecution, and most probably continued for some time, without molestation, in the peaceable exercise of his ministry.

Brook might here have added a fact, recorded by Hackett, that Ward was so good a friend to the Church of England, that he was the means of retaining several persons who were wavering about conformity, within the pale of the Episcopal communion.

After eleven years of comparative quiet, Ward was prosecuted again for alleged nonconformity, at the instigation of Archbishop

Laud. Prynne, in his account of Laud's trial (p. 361), tells us that, in the year 1635, he was impeached in the High Commission Court for preaching against bowing at the name of Jesus, and against the *Book of Sports*, and for having said 'that the Church of England was ready to ring changes in religion', and 'that the gospel stood on tip-toe ready to be gone'. He was found guilty, was enjoined to make a public recantation in such form as the Court should appoint, and condemned in costs of the suit. Upon his refusal to recant, he was committed to prison, where he remained a long time.

In a note to Brook's account of this disgraceful transaction, which he appears to have gathered out of Rushworth's *Collections* and Wharton's *Troubles of Laud*, he mentions a remarkable fact about Ward at this juncture of his life, which shows the high esteem in which he was held at Ipswich. It appears that after his suspension the Bishop of Norwich would have allowed his people another minister in his place; but 'they would have Mr Ward, or none'!

The last four years of Ward's life are a subject on which I find it very difficult to discover the truth. Brook says that, after his release from prison, he retired to Holland, and became a colleague of William Bridge, the famous Independent minister of Yarmouth, who had settled at Rotterdam. He also mentions a report that he and Mr Bridge renounced their Episcopal ordination, and were reordained, – 'Mr Bridge ordaining Mr Ward, and Mr Ward returning the compliment'. He adds another report, that Ward was unjustly deposed from his pastoral office at Rotterdam, and after a short interval restored.

I venture to think that this account must be regarded with some suspicion. At any rate, I doubt whether we are in possession of all the facts in the transaction which Brook records. That Ward retired to Holland after his release from prison is highly probable. It was a step which many were constrained to take for the sake of peace and liberty of conscience, in the days of the Stuarts. That he was pastor of a church at Rotterdam, in conjunction with Bridge, that differences arose between him and his colleague, that he was temporarily deposed from his office and afterward restored, are things which I think very likely.

His reordination is a point which I think questionable. For one thing it seems to me exceedingly improbable, that a man of Ward's age and standing would first be reordained by Bridge, who was twenty-three years younger than himself, and afterward reordain Bridge. For another thing, it appears very strange that a man who had renounced his episcopal orders, should have afterwards received an honourable burial in the aisle of an Ipswich church, in the year 1639. One thing only is clear. Ward's stay at Rotterdam could not have been very lengthy. He was not committed to prison till 1635, and was buried in 1639. He 'lay in prison long', according to Prynne. At any rate, he lay there long enough to write a Latin work, called *A Rapture*, of which it is expressly stated that it was composed during his imprisonment 'in the Gate House'. In 1638, we find him buying a house in Ipswich. It is plain, at this rate, that he could not have been very long in Holland.

However, all the transactions at Rotterdam, so far as Ward is concerned, are involved in some obscurity. Stories against eminent Puritans were easily fabricated and greedily swallowed in the seventeenth century. Brook's assertion that Ward died in Holland, about 1640, is so entirely destitute of foundation, that it rather damages the value of his account of Ward's latter days.

Granting, however, that after his release from prison Ward retired to Holland, there seems every reason to believe that he returned to Ipswich early in 1638. It appears from the town books of Ipswich (according to Wodderspoon), that, in April

1638, he purchased the house provided for him by the town for £140, repaying the contributors the sum contributed by them. He died in the month of March 1639, aged 62; and was buried in St Mary-le-Tower, Ipswich, on the 8th of that month. A certified copy of the entry of his burial, in the parish register, is in my possession. On a stone which was laid in his lifetime in the middle aisle of the church, the following words (according to Clarke's *History of Ipswich*) are still extant –

> Watch, Ward! yet a little while,
> And he that shall come will come.

Under this stone it is supposed the bones of the good old Puritan preacher were laid; and to this day he is spoken of by those who know his name in Ipswich as 'Watch Ward.'

It only remains to add, that Ward married, in 1604, a widow named Deborah Bolton, of Isleham in Cambridge, and had by her a family.[5] It is an interesting fact, recorded in the town-books of Ipswich, that after his death, as a mark of respect, his widow and his eldest son Samuel were allowed for their lives the stipend enjoyed by their father, viz., £100 annually. It is also worthy of remark, that he had two brothers who were ministers, John and Nathaniel. John Ward lived and died rector of St Clement's, Ipswich; and there is a tablet and short inscription about him in that church. Nathaniel Ward was minister of Stardon, Herts, went to America in 1634, returned to England in 1646, and died at Shenfield, in Essex, 1653.

[5] For this fact, and the facts about Ward's degrees at Cambridge, I am indebted to a well-informed writer in *Notes and Queries* for October 1861.

There is an excellent portrait of Ward still extant in Ipswich, in the possession of Mr Hunt, solicitor. He is represented with an open book in his right hand, a ruff round his neck, a peaked beard and moustaches. On one side is a coast beacon lighted; and there is an inscription –

Watche Ward. Ætatis suæ 43. 1620.

The following extract, from a rare volume called *The Tombstone; or, a notice and imperfect monument of that worthy man Mr John Carter, Pastor of Bramford and Belstead in Suffolk* (1653), will probably be thought to deserve insertion as an incidental evidence of the high esteem in which Ward was held in the neighbourhood of Ipswich. The work was written by Mr Carter's son; and the extract describes what occurred at his father's funeral. He says (at pages 26–7):

In the afternoon, February 4, 1634, at my father's interring, there was a great confluence of people from all parts thereabout, ministers and others taking up the word of Joash, King of Israel, 'O my father! my father! the chariots of Israel and the horsemen thereof!' Old Mr Samuel Ward, *that famous divine, and the glory of Ipswich* came to the funeral, brought a mourning gown with him, and offered very respectfully to preach the funeral sermon, seeing that such a congregation was gathered together, and upon such an occasion. But my sister and I durst not give way to it; for our father had often charged us in his lifetime, and upon his blessing, that no service should be at his burial. For, said he, 'It will give occasion to speak some good things of me that I deserve not, and so false things will be uttered in this pulpit.' Mr Ward rested satisfied, and did forbear. But the next Friday, at Ipswich, he turned his whole lecture into a funeral sermon for my father, in which he did lament and honour him, to the great satisfaction of the whole auditory.

I have now brought together all that I can discover about Samuel Ward's history. I heartily regret that the whole amount is so small, and that the facts recorded about him are so few. But we must not forget that the best part of Ward's life was spent in Suffolk, and that he seldom left his own beloved pulpit in St Mary-le-Tower, Ipswich.[6] That he was well known by reputation beyond the borders of his own county, there can be no doubt.

His selection to be a preacher at St Paul's Cross, in 1616, is a proof of this. But it is vain to suppose that the reputation of

[6] It seems that he expounded half the Bible during his ministry in Ipswich! See his preface to *The Happiness of Practice*.

a preacher, however eminent, who lives and dies in a provincial town, will long survive him. In order to become the subject of biographies, and have the facts of his life continually noted down, a man must live in a metropolis. This was not Ward's lot; and, consequently, at the end of four hundred years, we seem to know little about him.

It only remains to say something about the *Sermons and Treatises*, which are now reprinted, and made accessible to the modern reader of theology. It must be distinctly understood that they do not comprise the whole of Ward's writings. Beside these he wrote, in conjunction with Yates, a reply to Montague's famous book, *Appello Cæsarem*. There is also reason to think that he published one or two other detached sermons beside those which are now reprinted. I think, however, there can be little doubt that those now republished are the only works of Samuel Ward which it would have been worth while to reprint, and in all probability the only works which he himself would have wished to be reproduced.

Of the merits of these sermons, the public will now be able to form an opinion. They were thought highly of in time past, and have received the commendation of very competent judges. Fuller testifies that Ward 'had a sanctified fancy, dexterous in designing expressive pictures, representing much matter in a little model'.

Doddridge says that Ward's 'writings are worthy to be read through. His language is generally proper, elegant, and nervous. His thoughts are well digested, and happily illustrated. He has many remarkable veins of wit. Many of the boldest figures of speech are to be found in him, beyond any English writer, especially apostrophes, prosopopœias, dialogisms, and allegories.' This praise may at first sight seem extravagant. I shall, however, be disappointed if those who take the trouble to read Ward's writings do not think it well deserved.

The *doctrine* of Ward's sermons is always thoroughly evangelical. He never falls into the extravagant language about repentance, which disfigures the writings of some of the Puritans. He never wearies us with the long supra-scriptural, systematic statements of theology, which darken the pages of others. He is always to the point, always about the main things in divinity, and generally sticks to his text. To exalt the Lord Jesus Christ as high as possible, to cast down man's pride, to expose the sinfulness of sin, to spread out broadly and fully the remedy of the gospel, to awaken the unconverted sinner and alarm him, to build up the true Christian and comfort him, – these seem to have been objects which Ward proposed to himself in every sermon. And was he not right? Well would it be for the churches if we had more preachers like him!

The *style* of Ward's sermons is always eminently simple. Singularly rich in illustration, – bringing every day life to bear continually on his subject, – pressing into his Master's service the whole circle of human learning, – borrowing figures and similes from everything in creation, – not afraid to use familiar language such as all could understand, – framing his sentences in such a way that an ignorant man could easily follow him, – bold, direct, fiery, dramatic, and speaking as if

he feared none but God, he was just the
man to arrest attention, and to keep it
when arrested, to set men thinking, and
to make them anxious to hear him again.
Quaint he is undoubtedly in many of his
sayings. But he preached in an age when
all were quaint, and his quaintness probably struck no-one as remarkable. Faulty
in taste he is no doubt. But there never
was the popular preacher against whom
the same charge was not laid. His faults,
however, were as nothing compared to his
excellencies. Once more I say, well would it
be for the churches if we had more preachers like him!

The *language* of Ward's sermons ought
not to be passed over without remark. I
venture to say that, in few writings of the
seventeenth century, will there be found so
many curious, old-fashioned, and forcible

words as in Ward's sermons. Some of these words are unhappily obsolete and unintelligible to the multitude, to the grievous loss of English literature. Many of them would require explanatory footnotes, in order to make them understood by the majority of readers.

I now conclude by expressing my earnest hope that the scheme of republication may meet with the success which it deserves, and that the writings of men like Samuel Ward may be read and circulated throughout the land. I wish it for the sake of the Puritan divines.[7] We owe them a debt, in Great

---

[7] To regard the Puritans of the seventeenth century, as some appear to do, as mere ranting enthusiasts, is nothing better than melancholy ignorance. Fellows and heads of colleges, as many of them were, they were equal, in point of learning, to any divines of their day. To say that they were mistaken in some of their opinions, is one thing; to speak of them as 'unlearned and ignorant men' is simply absurd, and flatly contrary to facts.

Britain, which has never yet been fully paid. They are not valued as they deserve, I firmly believe, because they are so little known.

I wish it for the sake of the Protestant Churches of my own country, of every name and denomination. It is vain to deny that we have fallen on trying times for Christianity. Heresies of the most appalling kind are broached in quarters where they might have been least expected. Principles in theology which were once regarded as thoroughly established are now spoken of as doubtful matters. In a time like this, I believe that the study of some of the great Puritan divines is eminently calculated, under God, to do good and stay the plague. I commend the study especially to all young ministers. If they want to know how powerful minds and mighty intellects can think out deep theological subjects, arrive at decided conclusions, and yet give implicit reverence to the Bible, let them read Puritan divinity.

I fear it is not a reading age. Large books, especially, have but little chance of a perusal. Hurry, superficiality, and bustle are the characteristics of our times. Meagreness, leanness, and shallowness are too often the main features of modern sermons. Nevertheless, something must be attempted in order to check existing evils. The churches must be reminded that there can be no really powerful preaching without deep thinking, and little deep thinking without hard reading.

The republication of our best Puritan divines I regard as a positive boon to the church and the world, and I heartily wish it God speed.